When It Comes to Love

a collection of poems

Rama Kaba

Zirc⬥n Press

WHEN IT COMES TO LOVE

Copyright © 2018, 2015 by Rama Kaba

All rights reserved.
No part of this publication may be reproduced, distributed, or transmitted in any form or by any means, including copying, recording, or other electronic or mechanical methods, without the prior written permission of the publisher, except in the case of brief quotations embodied in critical reviews and certain other noncommercial uses permitted by copyright law.

For permission requests, email info@zirconpress.com
"Attention: Rights & Permissions."

ISBN 978-0-9809432-7-6 (paperback)
ISBN 978-0-9809432-9-0 (hardcover)
ISBN 978-0-9809432-3-8 (ebook)

Published by Zircon Press
Cover and Interior illustrations by Ania Van Minnen
Cover and Interior Designs by Alex Damianidis

First Printing Edition, 2015
Second Printing Edition, 2018

www.zirconpress.com

When It Comes To Love

Ania Van Minnen

for anyone who has ever loved

When It Comes to Love

ACKNOWLEDGEMENTS

The idea to re-publish this book with a new cover came about earlier this year when I found myself no longer happy with the original cover. The ridiculously pink cover represented a younger me, which made sense when I originally published it back in 2015. Also, a lot of the poems in this collection were published over several decades. But so much has changed since publishing my second book that I wanted to give my first book the same chance to reach a wider audience that might have been turned off by the overly girly pink cover.

This time around, a very special thanks to an amazing artist, Ania Van Minnen, who took the time out of her busy schedule to draw me some beautiful flowers. And of course, thanks to my wonderful husband again, master graphic designer, for editing the interior and exterior of this book and for being patient with me again, as I bossed him around.

A special thanks to Dunja Baus for being the best editor ever, and to everyone who has supported my love for poetry and encouraged me to never give up being a poet.

And most importantly, to the wonderful readers who are buying my books and reading my words. Thank you, thank you.

CONTENTS

SOME WHERE IN TIME

Somewhere in Time...•3•
What Have You Done...•4•
Take It Back..•5•
Daddy...•7•
Cancun...•8•
Passion...•9•
A Touch..•10•
Like The Sun..•11•
The Artist's Treat..•12•
If I Was Your Man..•13•
Rosa..•15•
The Rain...•17•
Tell The World..•18•
Sunday at Coney Island..•19•
Tell Me...•21•
Undone...•22•

WHEN YOU WALKED AWAY

When You Walked Away......................................•27•
A Broken Heart Near Devils River.......................•28•
Today..•29•
Let It Not Be Said..•30•
Breathe...•31•
A Moment..•33•
People Leaving...•34•
Liquid Lies...•36•
Rich..•37•

Broken	•38•
My Family	•40•
Those Kinds of Goodbyes	•41•
Still	•43•
The Season	•44•
What I'll Never Say	•46•
Enough	•48•
The Night	•49•
Return	•51•
The Art of Pretending	•52•
Rain	•54•
Break	•55•

AFTER THE STORM

After The Storm	•59•
Those Silent Words	•60•
Love is a Terrible Thing	•61•
Lovers' Rendezvous	•64•
Carpe Diem	•66•
The Morning	•67•
You	•69•
Kissing Stars	•71•
Shapes	•72•
I Still Think of You	•73•
Perfection	•74•
Captured	•75•
Again	•76•
Mine	•77•
Share	•79•
Whole	•80•
All I Want	•81•
Celestial	•82•

HAIKU POEMS

Now and Forever .... •85•
Destiny .... •86•
Sun and Moon .... •87•
When We are Old .... •88•
The Price .... •89•
Float .... •90•
What is Mine .... •91•
Joy .... •92•
If You Loved Me .... •93•

*Our thoughts anchored by the moon,
we pleaded our spirits into existence.*

_Perfection

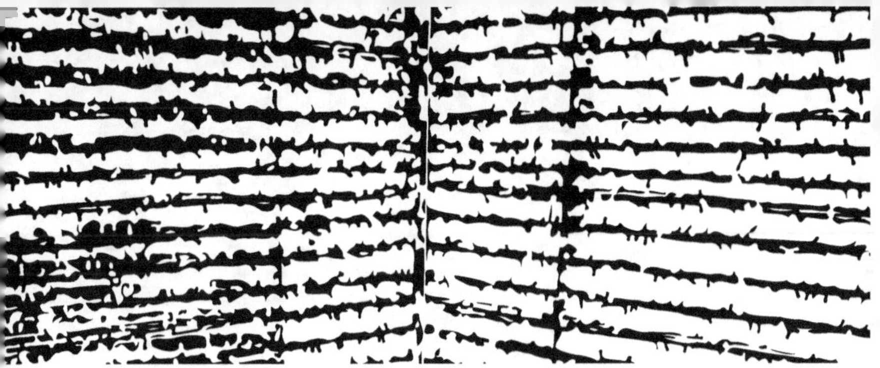

SOME WHERE IN TIME

SOMEWHERE IN TIME

Somewhere in time
I would erase finality,
so you could always be mine.

Our rebirth is inconsequential;
I would recognize you
when you cease to breathe.

Somewhere in time
I would fade the centuries,
so you could always be mine.

The petty games death plays are irrelevant;
absolution is ours in the final days.

Somewhere in time
I would embrace Abaddon,
for you should be mine, always.

WHAT HAVE YOU DONE

that caterpillars twirl and whirl
madly out of their cocoons?

What do you say about:
the sleepless nights;
the rushed mornings;
the sluggish seconds that evolve into minutes—
what do they mean?

What have you done to make
smiles spread across lips, cheeks,
and crinkle in the corner of my eyes?
And what have you to say
about the belly-clenching laughter?

What have you done to make
joy mingle easily with fear?
Pain is nonexistent as bodies entwine like vine leaves
and violently explode…

What have you done to make
battles worth fighting—
life worth living.

What have you done to make
death worth embracing…

TAKE IT BACK

I don't like it one bit.
I can't control it.
No air without him.
I don't want this feeling
or this insufferable period of waiting.

Patience will never be my forte.

Freedom, I can't seem to conjure;
a traitor in my midst.
My unconscious brevity collides with thoughts of him—

Why me? Why now?
Why this feeling?
This lackadaisical feeling
eats pieces of me.

My hands shake like crumbs.
My heart, my head, my…
What more is there to say?

The bones in my finger long since mollified uncertainty.
I can't grasp my chest;
I'm forgetting
to live.

Why me? Why him?
Nothing special, but yet, yet
somehow my heart yearns for his "what ifs."

"What if I'm the best thing that will ever happen to you?"
"What if I'm your one and you let me go?"
"What if, what if, you jump and I catch you?"
"What if…"

I don't want it.
I never asked for it.
Take it back.
Take it back.

Please,
take it back.

DADDY

Daddy.
Da—Di.
Take me in your arms and swing me around and swing me around, and around till time unravels and I'm nine forever. Swing me around and around till disappointments and failed prayers never venture forth. Oh keep swinging me around till morning turns to dusk, and still my head is muzzled with content for simply, for simply making me dizzy and giddy in swing.

Daddy.
Oh, da—di, da—di, da—di,
don't you know how much I love thee.
Even, even when you say I'm too big to sit on your lap.
Even, even when I can never tell you about the blood.
Even and even when I can no longer look you in the eye.
And even and even and even if you cannot see what could have been, I'm still your little girl.

CANCUN

The sea is dead;
lifeless in its vast openness.
The wind embraces the prickly hair on my arms.
The sea is alive.
The sun grazes and scratches its surface.
I can't believe I'm here.
I see the truth:
> the sky, the birds;
> the wind, the sun;
> the crispness in the air;
> the sand between my toes;
> the heat between my thighs.

I want to show you
the party in Cancun.

PASSION

Passion is not volume,
but rather the soul bearing dusk
that echoes an omniscient creator.

Passion is not visible,
but it is the quiddity of lost myths and legends
the heart needs to feel to sustain its existence.

Passion is the mother
that holds and feeds her child close to her breast,
so her milk nourishes those essential primary needs.

Passion is the wrinkles that ripple and crinkle
around one's body revealing mortality,
time, and the fleetingness of life.

Passion is the metacognition of living:
memories firmly stacked upon each other,
an archive of moments, elapsed.

A TOUCH

I want to hold your hand,
trace the lines curving your palm
to the edge of your opisthenar.

I want to touch fingertips to tips,
index to index, erasing the division between
your brain's left and right hemispheres.

I want to blur those lines
so your finer motor skill is at ease
to see me flush;

to know that with just one stroke
I am yours.

LIKE THE SUN

Scorching sky
holds rouge et orange hues.

Your warmth,
pressing,
caressing,
easing
into the horizon.

Incarcerated and enchanted
by your glaze,
you set, I follow.

THE ARTIST'S TREAT

Secretly yours in a primitive beat.
Our virgin bodies precede their production
as our skins generate indispensable heat.

This is the cadence of an artistic vital seduction—
touch, taste, tease—we are complete.

Feel these lines and curves
as an introduction to an open valley.

Come...

Modesty is not required.
I want it known that your kisses destroy my wits.

Let us repeat the strokes
that broke an artist's construction.

I would not mind a public performance
since your love is truly a treat.

IF I WAS YOUR MAN

If I was your man,
I would hold you in my arms as you fall
      asleep
and whisper that my existence is solely based
on your calm perception—
      if only you were mine.

I would grow flowers that causally pass death as they reap
their seeds for your impending conception.
If I was your man,
I would hold you in my arms as you fall
      asleep.

I would kiss shadows on your cheeks
as the stars try to cheat
you out of the luminous warmth in your reception—
      if only you were mine.

I would watch for the tinting of your skin
as you weep with joy.
When it comes to pleasure, you would feel no exception.
If I was your man,
I would hold you in my arms as you fall
      asleep.

I would grab the right to peep into your dreams so you wouldn't fall prey to inception—
> if only you were mine.

I would caress your hair behind your ears
as I would part a heap of people crowding your presence;
you would never encounter deception.

If I was your man,
I would hold you in my arms as you fall
> asleep—
>> but if only you were mine.

ROSA

Oh Rosa,
where have you been?
I have been searching for you.

Come to me, Rosa!
The wind is gathering its strength,
while the snow ponders its coldness.

I see your thorn is still pricking hearts asunder.

It's cold outside, Rosa.
Last night's snow formed icy frames around my windows.

I can't see you anymore,
creeping tall and bright;
the sun glistering on your different scented hues.

Come inside Rosa,
and let me rub some attar onto your skin.

Let me count your petals:

Five petals for five days of winter;
I sat and waited for you.

Sniffing;
rubbing you across my face;
counting you:

"She loves me, she loves me not."
 Oh Rosa,
what have I done wrong
that you would end on such a note?

Have I not given you
red for passion?
White for affection?
Pink for sympathy?
Yellow for caring?
Peach for desire?

Rosa, my sweet dear—

Please come to me!

THE RAIN

Water tickles down your body...
I follow the thirst that cannot be quenched.
I hunger for your silkiness and your wetness.

Your innocence wanes in the cool mist.
You know how I feel about the rain—
it touches the places I long to taste.

Oh, to be the rain
enveloped between the battles
of angels' tears and demons' drool.

Flickering raindrops flame your hidden spots
in a gentle but shameless caress,
touching you in ways I only dream of.

To be, ah, to be this rain.

TELL THE WORLD

If I could tell the world,   I would.

    My hand secretly reaches for yours.

You smile, I come undone.

If I could tell the world,   I would.

Though how can they not see
that our eyes never fail to meet.

I would,   if I could tell the world,

      but nobody knows; nobody needs to know.

When somebody knows,

              everything ceases to matter.

SUNDAY AT CONEY ISLAND

Sunday morning
lover came to get me.
Parked his car in my driveway
for the long D ride.
We passed Grand Concourse;
found hair braiding along 125th St.;
missed nannies exploit black cards at Columbus Circle.
At 7th Ave., he squeezed my knee.
We glided by shame through Rockefeller Center.
Nothing happened either at New Utrecht Ave.

Sunday morning
Lover grabbed my hand.
His fingers spread and claimed the spaces between mine.
He squeezed my breath
as we took baby steps
toward Deno's Wonder Wheel.

Sunday morning
Lover held my arms.
Swirling and twirling and swinging,
we took rides and he won the prize:
we entered the fun house
but never saw our reflection.

Sunday morning
Lover put our shoes aside
on the boardwalk, and like children
left inside for too long,
we ran.
If we had a place to go, we would have ran there too.
We swam around dirty water and jellyfish;
we played with our feet and wiggled our toes.
I did not mind when he lifted me up
and clenched my waist.

Sunday morning
Lover made me an offer:
"Live forever in my arms darling,"
as he wiped the cotton candy residue
from my cheeks at the Teddy Bear booth.

I wish I could, I wish I might…

Sunday morning
I let Lover have it
because it was the only thing
I had to give the only thing
I could give

at Coney Island.

TELL ME

Tell me what you want from me.

Tell me how it's going to be.

Tell me what to do.

No, no, no…

I want you

to tell me

what you need

from me.

It's the only way expectations
won't grow into accusations.

The only way
these old bones won't rattle
when you finally take me into your arms.

UNDONE

When my eyes draw your smile
or my lips move your ears,
more than words are left unsaid.
You bedim temptation—
but still, when I look at you,
I come undone.

Honestly, my feelings remain unclear.
During the day, I could slap you silly
for placing me in this restless situation.
But at night, I could easily erase those marks.

For you, I would do anything and everything.
I would be yours—for as little as you could give me.
Because when you look at me,
I come undone.

You say I'm bad
because I refuse to not answer your calls.
I want to let it ring.
I want to expose you for what you are…,
but I don't.
Every little bit of you counts.

You're right, I'm no good.

But I'm another kind of Eve
that cuts and wears her shame.
Because when you whisper her name,
I just pretend you're calling me.

WHEN YOU WALKED AWAY

TODAY

I might not have to face today,
although the same was spoken yesterday.
I will not step toward tomorrow.

> i will sit and prepare
> while the rain purifies the air
>
> i will sit and stare
> while my tears wash my dirty hair
>
> i will sit and declare
> a lonely life which is most unfair
>
> i will sit and repair
> the endless nights that my eyes bare
>
> i will sit and compare
> all of my previous affairs

I might not have to face today,
although the same was spoken yesterday.
Tomorrow, I will not step toward.

LET IT NOT BE SAID

Let it not be said
that I have never given you all that you merit,
that I have never stood in front of you—incomplete,
my heart on a golden platter
while your eyes shone with power.

Let it not be said
that I have never loved you
until we reached the end of the universe.
Oh, how I held your hands,
dropped to my knees
and begged you.
I begged you till I turned raw
to never keep your spirit from me,
to never slash my core in half.

Let it not be said
that I have never forgiven,
even when it was all said and done,
even when there was nothing left of me
to give.

WHEN YOU WALKED AWAY

I do not know this feeling.
This restlessness and fearfulness
turns my stomach like rotten eggs,
and slothfully clenches my intestines.

My glorious reflection tumbles
and crumbles a river's surface asunder.
When you look away—
the turn of your head shifts the earth's axis.

An imbalance of stored emotions
quiver the greatest battle
between my tears and my worth,
and drown in luminous hopes and failed wishes.

As your hand slips from mine,
a part of me skips through time.
Your mercurial nature gets lost
in poignant agonies of waves.

Your hollow glaze burns into mine
like morning fog, blinding me—
still, I fall short in love's gain.
I lose,
               when you walk away.

A BROKEN HEART NEAR DEVILS RIVER

    Sometimes, Love doesn't always love you.

What's left of your heart turns blue
and blows across Devils River.
Feet sluggishly slap their beat
while water turns your cheeks askew.

Bluebonnets dance and stain your sheet.
The brightness of the sun's adieu
resembles Whitewater river.

Is it true you mournfully promulgated on Long Street?
Every words he said replays itself
and rushes in a melancholic birth.

    Love doesn't always love you.

Rugged streams stroke heartbreak anew,
while your reflection passes through Devils' remoteness.

You repeat past mistakes.
You forget like yesterday morning.
You're incomplete.

    Sometimes, love doesn't always love you.

BREATHE

Waiting,
patiently.

Loneliness is skulking around
the corner of my eyes.
"Please do not blink!"
"Try not to—"
I've been through worse than this.

Breathe
Breathe

Although I can't compare past mistakes,
I know better. I'm strong.
Strength is all I have
to bear these painful memories.

Breathe
Breathe

Wait,
I keep waiting.
Every word you say
cuts me deeply
slices and dices M E

Breathe
Breathe

"I sure can do this;
of course, I can do this!"

I've been through this before:
13, Daddy left
20, Mama left

Breathe
Breathe

Now that I'm older,
I don't want promises.

Breathe
Breathe

When you leave,
there'll be nothing of me
to give...

But somewhere between you leaving
and preparing myself for you leaving,

I forgot
to exhale.

A MOMENT

Immortality; I give up.
Love—discard.

Don't skip, my heart.
I can never count your worth.

My existence is abridging,
fearing endless nights, counting empty days—

I'm slowly

                f a d

                                i n g

a w

                a y.

PEOPLE LEAVING

Daddy leaving.

So much to be said, but my teeth scrape my tongue so poorly, a goodbye isn't even attempted. Nothing comes out. I stand there and can't say the words I slowly prepared two nights ago when I tripped over his worn-out yellow suitcase.

Even now, shame still follows me home. Its intensity becomes my fame. Disgrace: my reflection loves to hurl at me. A dagger delivers a smoother pain. Because when it happened, when he left that is, my young heart was frayed out of my flat chest and left on the floor to bleed.

Sounds dramatic, but true. I had to wipe the mess afterwards, so I would know. I still remember when I dropped the knife while my wrist leisurely bled—of course it had to be slow, so I could rethink my actions, after all I still had Mamma.

Mamma leaving.

So much to say, but the beginning shattered my speech. You would think I'd learned, but those old, old pain stops the lessons to be gained. I thought I'd be better this time; thought, this time around I'd be ready. Nobody else is left after all.

I tried to reach out, ask why—when she takes her bags as my young feet pester closer than her shadows. My hands were still too small to clutch her arm firmly. My knees scratched from crawling on the floor. Did I beg? Hell yes! Did I plead? Hell fucking yes! Didn't I mention my knees turned raw? I hold on to the belt on her red second-hand suitcase. But that used suitcase just lands on the ground, crashing with her useless goodbyes.

Loneliness still creeps behind me, waiting and dancing to the "Saddest Goodbyes." Wait—there's more…

But it's cool because I just learned to leave first.

LIQUID LIES

The glass is half empty,
but often, it's empty
because I keep to the bottle.

I drink your lies,
swallow my lies,
how bitter they taste.

I'm not over you.

RICH

I collect tears like pennies;
make wishes never to be granted.
Oh sunshine,
won't you give me a fraudulent smile;
make me jump high in Double Dutch.
But let the ropes touch me.
I want to lose in this game too;
my wallet can't fit in my purse.

BROKEN

Saddest of all is watching you go.
You walked away without looking back
to see if I'm stealing looks.

I know I was reckless,
but the facts remain: you hurt me.
Shockingly, you were always civil.

But on that day you left
I didn't cry.
I carried those damn tears
for months until they flaked into ashes.

I thought I was all,
but my image imitates nothingness;
those reflection of hollow pieces.

How do I go on,
when I can't collect myself
for a love that's gone?

I was dimwitted letting you go so easily.
You must have thought your love meant—nothing,
an empty shell left ashore.

I was a surly girl, proud of myself,
so sure that you'd come back,
I never followed.

MY FAMILY

There used to be four,
then there were three.
We never lingered on two,
went straight to one.

THOSE KINDS OF GOODBYES

It's been long.
Prehistoric emotions stay ashore.
The tranquil wave increases its altitude
while my toes wiggle in soft sands—
reminds me of unresolved decisions
left buried.

So long…
Time is never-ending;
its slow abundance of seconds ticks loudly.
My legs twitch to a tribal dance
underneath the sun's ray.
I saw you.

Somehow,
your eyes have lost the obscurity
they used to reside in whenever they smeared mine.
Your smiles now crunch at the corners of your eyes.
Heartbreaking to know I am not yours.
I left you.

Sometime,
after the storm, the sun cleared through.
A light shines, my purpose is finally clear:
An enlightening truth that our parting was for the best,

where before I never saw a future
without you—until now.

Finally,
You come toward me;
your arms reach out—my chest chokes, my eyes blur,
but I sniff hard and spread my lips wider than the Amazon.
I hold you in my arms—
nothing

The clearing:
I loved you once.
For that, I will keep you in Memory.
As a treasure, I will bury your lies.
Maybe at times, I will permit grief a brief visit,
when I think of you, you before your lies,
and me, in front of my eyes.

STILL

My heart shatters
into uncountable pieces.
I lie and reiterate your words;
I'm still flabbergasted
by how tactless they were.

THE SEASON

I gather your smiles while the leaves change their hues.
Warm oranges camouflaged our soulless ground
as the wind and the bare trees offer esoteric clues
about a reconciliation that long since drowned.

In the mirth of Fall, you gather me into your festive arms,
the coldness slowly creeping in my soul remains at bay
as your touch reveals another one of your charms,
and your eyes display the events of our confining days.

Winter creeps among my shelter in your embrace,
and snow falls, and polishes the faces of lonesome beings.
During festivities, I splatter kisses on your face:
your eyes, nose, cheeks, and lips are worth sightseeing.

But when the zealous snow mountains start
to melt like rivers streaming muddy distress,
my forgiveness for your discretions depart
the slushy snow that confesses Spring's progress.

Spring, battles cold mornings, sunny days, and colder nights—
our relationship and the temperature still remains unclear.
But I do have shorter nights to reminisce and fight
my never-ending emotions as longer days adhere

to the birds singing praises about Mother Earth.
Restraint befriends me, as I return your smile.
I have hope that those rainy days would rebirth
a final resolution. But Summer fashions a style

of hunger as your licentious eyes
warm my skin—I am pathetic. I let the sun's glare
enflame my weakness. And so, I tell you lies:
I let my nonexistent affairs fly in the humid air,

hoping you would end the image of what we used to be.
But once again, the trees begin to undress,
as the wind gathers its strength to free
those bitter emotions we continue to compress.

WHAT I'LL NEVER SAY

Soft words spoken in an unforgiving tongue—
I wish to travel in a backward beginning
to the day I let your hands slip from mine
into a bitter chaos of colliding pain.

This shattered heart of mine is still beating,
has flooded itself with more rain than New Orleans.
I'm esurient for what I once held,
enmeshed since the beginning of time.

I long,
I long to be forgiven.
I long,
I long to be loved.
But when I see you look at her,
your lips cosset hers…

I could live without you;
I try to deceive myself,
but my lies hurl at me faster than a pitcher's strike.
I'm sorry,
my heart misses its other half.

To your face, to your eyes
I want to say what's in my heart,
but to your face and to your eyes,
I save all the things I'll never say.

Maybe someday,
when the thought of without you
is a greater pain than with you
I'll say what I'll never say.

ENOUGH

At 3 pm,
you ask
if I had ever
loved you.

                                              You looked into my eyes.

At 3:01,
you packed
your bags
and left.

THE NIGHT

The icy silence of darkness encloses me.
In a distance, I'm in a cocoon of boisterous sympathy—
a palpable fact, evident than an ineluctable destiny.

Fortune clenches my mind with nails
sharper than the White shark's teeth.
Nevertheless, I hold my tears
when love decides it no longer resides with me.

Love no longer sits with me at night,
or cherishes my desires while potbellied children
collect their fallen limbs and half eaten hearts.

The day—all the day ever does is try to palliate
those elongated sentiments of restlessness.
Those dreams of broken dolls with iniquitous blood,
drips and drips and drips.

I welcome the darkness;
it blazes my smashed heart afire—a reason to live
as I fancy being inveigled into demonic needs.
He squeezes and leaves my essence apart,
but I laugh with pain—ah, the joy, ah, to live
in his beaded eyes.

My hands coalesces into Darkness,
who understands my inner need, my thirst.

I know the quintessence of pain resides within the night.
Where else would it be?

After all, who can hide and mask my pain better than you?
Who is a better friend than you?

You, who welcomes me
in a bond sealed in true blood.

You, who shadows my secrets,
as I dance my heart out
into your darkness.

RETURN

He left
without a trace of himself,
of the something we once were.

There is nothing
to prove we were once lovers,
except, in the memories.

There, again and again, I rehash.
I know
I have lost him.

THE ART OF PRETENDING

Sing to me
slowly and softly,
a lullaby. Please.
Tickle me till my belly hurts.

Oh, my, am I bleeding?
Are you bleeding?
I thought you would keep me safe.
But danger—

I open my eyes,
the fairies are gone,
Lolita has left again,
or rather, I stopped believing…

But,
Mr. Rabbit is still missing one of his ears.

Sing to me,
slowly and softly,
hold me, carry me, please. Love me.
Oh, forgive me for I have sinned—
I need to pray again, he tells me.
I stopped believing—faith diminishes.
This isn't real, he tells me.
Reality is what you make of it, sweetie.

So what am I?
Am I unstable?
A stigma?
There is sickness in me.
What a fibber…

Sing to me,
don't stop. Never stop
the lullaby; I wish to be your baby
forever.
That danger cannot touch me.
Wait—
shut up, I hear something…

Sing to me,
go ahead, sing,
even if you don't know the words;
I don't know honesty without a taste of your lies.
There is no joy without that pinch of your pain.

Go ahead and sing to me.
Slowly and softly,
if you like.
Pretend that the shadow
never touched me.
Do it,
sing to me,
lie to me.
Try it.
But you can only sing for so long—
mother.

RAIN

I swear to Calypso that on the night you left it rained.
When I heard the door slam, I shattered.
The deadly songs of sirens compelled me
toward the edge—
I fell into the rain
so no one could see
me cry.

BREAK

Why is my reflection still residing in your eyes,
when you played me like a classic guitar
with only one string left?

Why are my kisses still leaving marks on your skin,
when you stretched me
out as if I was still made of rubber?

Why do you persist,
when you know I'm not strong
enough to walk away?

Please,
don't break me
too…

AFTER THE STORM

AFTER THE STORM

Nothing is ever more true
than when the clouds part ways
and the sun slowly peeks and shines
on the glistening skins of petals.

Nothing is lovelier
than the dew arriving after last night's rain
to bless the union of blossoms.
The last drop, the last drop

falls and impregnates the world anew
and nothing, nothing is ever more exact
than knowing that you love me
and I love you.

God had it right:
things are better after the storm.

THOSE SILENT WORDS

I will always remember it
like it was yesterday.
You took my hand
and off we went.
I could never love another.

I will always remember the first:
we stood together and spoke without words.
You gathered me close and our hips kissed.
You loved me with your dangerous lips.
I was yours and I did not mind.

I will always remember the last:
we stood apart and I said those silent words,
but your lips hissed those silent words.
I lost you and I did not mind.

No, I did not mind at all,
because if I did,
I would not have written this poem.

LOVE IS A TERRIBLE THING

Love is a terrible thing,
for when the heart breaks, it does so
in vague wishes blowing across the ocean.
The anguish and guilt of shameless thoughts part the sea,
revealing heartaches that cannot be glossed over
by charming blushes and flirtatious eyes.
It all starts with the never-ending wooing,
where sweet words are tossed about like rice.
But no one ever mentions how he tosses her like dice.
Nor do they acknowledge when her frantic heart
wants to indulge in dramatic tantrums.

When she starts to love again,
she ignores sincere advances and races across the floor
into any receiving arms.
She would take being varnish,
if it would mean feeling like satin.
She would gladly part with her possession—
objectify herself—if she never parts with love.
A cocoon of passion inflames and tosses
toward meaningless lovers;
the seduction glazes over her neediness,
as they whisper sweet words into her ears.

Love is a terrible thing,
for once the heart tastes it,
it reaches across space to unite two beings.

It is a continuous game
that starts many hearts racing and blind eyes seeking.
It starts outside the home;
in the bedroom, it ends.
It blurs distance;
for once the heart recognizes its kinship,
it travels across time.
A heart would sit and wait for its better half.
Neither wealth nor beauty can play a foul game.

Love in the end is a terrible thing,
for now that the heart has had a taste
it will wait and affirm its rightful heir—
a thousand unsettled wishes and soulful kisses
left unshared.

Love is a terrible thing,
for sure, when the heart stops beating
love will continue,
diffusing no patience for death,
and love will continue
until better souls meet half way.

Love is a terrible thing,
for once the heart experiences love,
it settles for no less;
contentment plays no part.

LOVERS' RENDEZVOUS

I search for you in the stars.
An extended sentiment left astray,
I weep with agony—it's true—
but my heart was never one to convey
what I hold dear.

To the known and the unknown,
I would allege my forlorn essence
in a timeless celebration
because in the end,
I only crave to portray a perpetual dedication.

The barefaced moon acts as my canvas,
I draw my newfound feelings.
I colored them gay.
The blue hue of my stretched misery slowly fades.
Its lingering shadows array my happiness
in a guarded cache.

In your eyes is a deep felt salvation,
the lonesomeness that still settles in the corner of my chest
crashes in an enduring birth.
I give to you in a bash, a perpetual dedication.

No doubts about the way my heart glue itself to yours.
The uncertainties no longer weigh on my brazen thoughts.
I no longer keep my desires at bay.

Your butterfly kisses are the start of my day;
they erupt my heart in a sensual vibration.
I hope and pray you would never dismay
a perpetual dedication.

At last, we finally meet again at a scintillating soirée;
our hands greet, I am in total fascination.
With all said and done, I will show you,
every day, a perpetual dedication.

CARPE DIEM

And I capture the love that lights
like a wakeful moon over the ocean.
And I capture your eyes, preparing flight
with wings that set my heart in motion.
And I capture the first sun. At great height
you and I will set the day.
And soon as our hearts start to run, our heartbeats recite
the life we hold while we sail across the bay.
And I capture Capella—even at night
to be with you in former times, for you make me laugh.
And I, oh how I love the charming knight
in you, because without you I'm truly daft.

THE MORNING

Sadness lurks around the corner
and offers shades of blackened pains.

Sadness befriends my shadows,
so I rush to stumble upon the morning light;
nobody but me and my thoughts.

A slow smile peeks through this cloudy perception
as I pen this place as my own,
as the shyness of morning light creeps itself
between the naked trees in my humble field.

The sentiment of relationships
that carries everlasting inconsistent emotions
has finally reached its quietus.

I'm not sad.

No, the shades of the morning dew
no longer distress me.

My heart is intact,
lighter than the fine lines
established between reality and foolishness.

I am satisfied.

I know the morning light
will brighten the darkness
trying to make a home
in me,
out of me,
on me.

YOU

You,
you catch me when I fall;
sometimes you drop me—
then pretend you never meant for it to happen.

You,
you dry my tears when I cry;
of course, sometimes you are the cause
of those unwanted tears and pains.

You,
you hold me when everyone lets me go;
sometimes too tightly,
but I know I can always count on you.

You,
you grow with me differently,
but then when it comes to you,
nothing ever goes according to plan.

You,
you sit with me while my heart rips;
let me not remind you, it was your idea
that caused this heartache in the first place.

You,
you stood beside me when everyone else left;
of course, you had to lecture me about
who my real friends are.

You,
you listen and watch as I bear myself,
not once did you let me get away with
sulking, but had me laughing in a second.

You,
you I can count on, time does not matter,
since you like calling me in the morning
just to remind me that you'll be calling me in the evening.

You,
you always forgive no matter how much it hurts;
you understand what others disregard;
you feel what others ignore;
you know me inside out.
Even if you are not answering my calls at the moment
I will still call you tomorrow,
and the day after, until you pick up.

You,
I know you can't ignore me forever.

KISSING STARS

We stood together under the sky,
while fireflies, too, embraced.
Leaning on the fence in front of my house,
your red Ford pickup shined in my driveway.
You took my hand; I took a stand.
I lifted on my tiptoe to kiss above your lips—
I caressed you senseless—between now and then
our lips touched.
I swear the world stopped spinning.
I swear the clouds tasted fear
when my arms snaked around your neck
and your arms enclosed my waist
as we kissed the stars.
Everything is all right.

SHAPES

Finally, your shy hand swooshes into mine.
I hold tight, for today, this time, everything is fine.

I have been waiting, seems like forever,
but forever only lasts through
the sadness and madness and happiness.

We toyed, bashfully fought, and still we would never
erase those wasteful life-teaching moments:

bloody shouts with walls vibrating sorrows,
losing count of broken dishes and teacups.

Still, you squeezed my hands when my mind disowned me;
I carried you when your body failed you;

you dried my tears and I've watered yours;
we weathered several storms over the years;

I built you a wall with blissfulness and giddiness,
even though you crudely crashed mine.

But it's okay.

I have been waiting, seems like forever,
to tell you I love you, even if I don't
recall the lines dressing your face.

I STILL THINK OF YOU

I still think of you, you and only you.
After all this time, even though it's overdue.
I still remember, an abandoned love that has my heart
chasing spirits in Eden. I still expose you as art—
such silkiness to your soul; my fingers colouring you blue.

I think about you, chasing thoughts only you knew;
I undress your features in a wanderlust hue.
When you left I forgave, even though I fell apart,
I still think of you.

And here's heaven shimmering with hope—I flew,
swaying to ceaseless memories. It's true
your image is marked in immortality. When a part
of you, ghostly, kisses me asleep, I start
to relinquish the life we once shared anew.
I still think of you.

PERFECTION

This is how it was meant to be . . .

Stars entwined like a sailor's knot,
we sailed across the Black Sea.

Our thoughts anchored by the moon,
we pleaded our spirits into existence.

A painter brushed free what's carved in stone—
what we forgo, but it always lingers:

that love is the climax of life.

CAPTURED

Memories captured in heart shaped frames.
My finger slowly traces your face—

I did that to you,
incarcerating your laughter and tears.

Your golden smiles beam over the years
on the light sensitive surface.

Though my lens could never colour your life,
memories are still gathered and created.

Though I only captured you today,
you are forever reflecting in permanence.

AGAIN

Yesterday is gone;

today is too late;

I'll wait till tomorrow

to love you

all over again.

MINE

Your eyes seek me.
I have memories to hold on to
for years, decades, centuries,
I'll hold to these declarations:

I swear I saw you, I held you;
I swear I kissed you, loved you;

I swear that I ran into your arms
and heaven was within reach.

Your soulful laughs touch me.
I hear your voice
for days, weeks, months,
I'll hold to these declarations:

I swear I chased you, found you;
I swear I danced with you, loved you;

I swear that I lay in your arms
and heaven was within reach.

Your graceful hands grab me.
I feel your skin
for seconds, minutes, hours
I'll hold to my declarations.

Though our paths have yet to cross,
our lives have yet to bear my vows,

I swear you are mine;
and I swear I am yours.

SHARE

Hold me tightly,
never let go.
My dreams are yours to wish upon,
my goals are yours to achieve,
my love is yours to cherish.

Hold me tightly,
never let go.
My life is yours to live,
my death is yours to die,
my soul is yours to sell.

Hold me tightly,
never let go.
My fears are yours to face,
my tears are yours to erase,
my shame is yours to replace.

Hold me tightly,
never let go,
I give myself freely to you,
entrust you to care for me,
and when you're old,
and you're done carrying me,
I'd have been carrying your share.

WHOLE

Love is standing still while the sun kisses your skin;
the wind caresses your hair as the brightness of the day
burns your loneliness away so that the joy within you
reveals the beauty of family as a golden ray.

Hope is stopping awhile to listen to the earth
as it deals with the myriad of unanswered expectations.
Let the beating of your heart collide with the birth
of celestial bliss and its never ending aspirations.

Faith is sailing across a tempestuous ocean
as its jealous waves tease the tranquillity of your soul.
The ones you love have given you their devotions
so that when you look across the sea,

                    the stillness makes you whole.

ALL I WANT

All I want
is to grow old in you;
travel the world with you;
sit beneath the sky and count the stars.

All I want
is to get lost in your eyes;
take a boat or a train ride;
erase those seconds
from ever reaching a minute.

All I want
is to exist, always, in your mind;
fall asleep in your strong arms,
but wake up to your charms;
and stop the earth from cracking.

All I want is to grow old in you,
be a part of you.
All I want
in this world
is you.

CELESTIAL

Do not seek me for yourself; I am immortal.
Do not let me be; I will fly away
with any chance of time to grab all that is mine.
In the past, future, or somewhere in time,
I am neither born nor dead.
But to the multi-minded,
I am the spirit that rises and falls.
I am the sun, the moon, the stars.
I hold time in my hand.

HAIKU POEMS

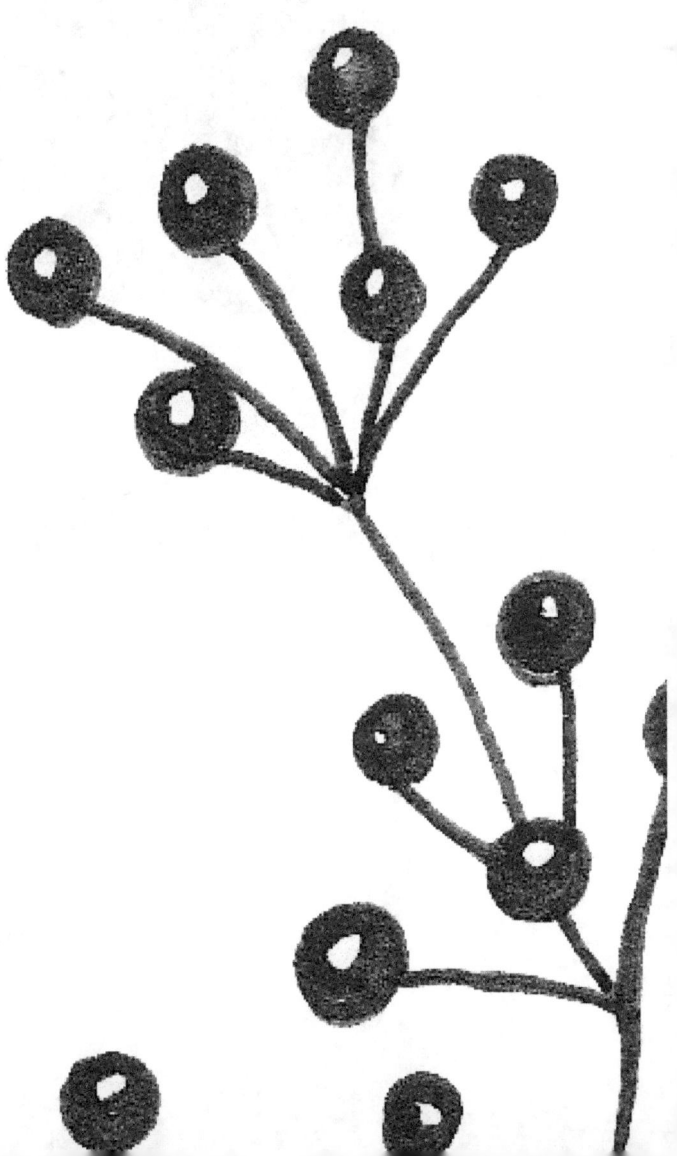

NOW AND FOREVER

i will carry you

when your body betrays you

now and forever

DESTINY

what is destiny?

hand in hand, eternity—

no end to true love

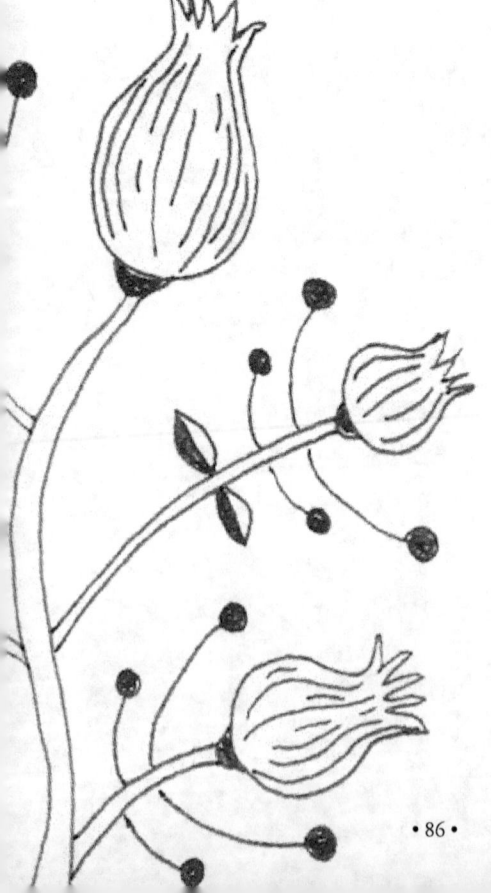

SUN AND MOON

i draw my last breath

and suck in the sun and moon

i love you this much

WHEN WE ARE OLD

when I look at you

i see us grey and merry

brushing lips to lips

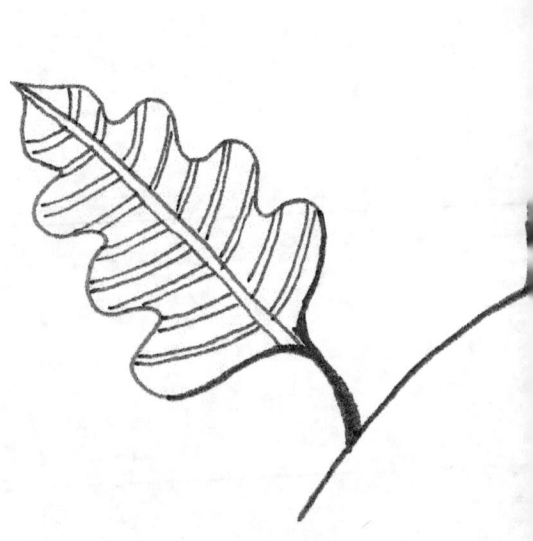

THE PRICE

this love is not free

loyalty and honesty

is the price you pay

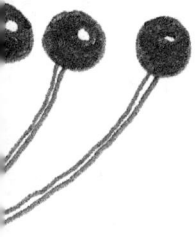

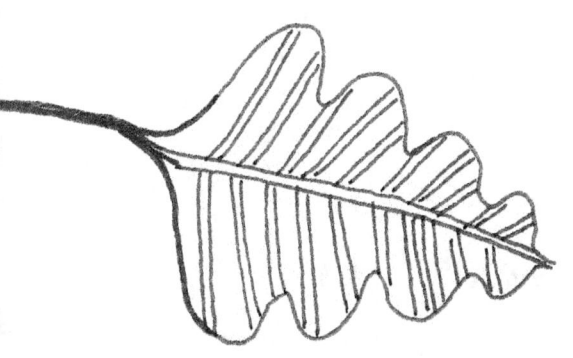

FLOAT

your hand brushes mine

      i'm

            floating

                      in

                              nebula

drifting in your light

WHAT IS MINE

i won't give you up

angels will have to fight me

to take what is mine

JOY

mercurial boy

laugh lines frame your mouth and eyes

we've lived with laughter

IF YOU LOVE ME

i would die over

a thousand death to be yours

if ever you ask

ABOUT THE AUTHOR

Rama Kaba grew up in the Bronx, New York City and Columbus, Georgia before settling in Ontario, Canada.

She obtained her Bachelor of Arts from York University, and her Master of Information from the University of Toronto to become a librarian.

She works at the Hamilton Public Library, where she gets to indulge herself in her love for books and meet new and interesting people.

If you would like to hear about Rama's upcoming projects, visit her at www.ramakaba.com.

You can also follow her on Twitter @ramakaba and Instagram @chez_rama.

If you've enjoyed this book, please review and share it with others.

For more information about Rama Kaba
visit www.ramakaba.com

For more information about Zircon Press
visit www.zirconpress.com

www.ingramcontent.com/pod-product-compliance
Lightning Source LLC
Chambersburg PA
CBHW052027290426
44112CB00014B/2415